The Cherry On Top

Chocolate Or Vanilla He's Still A Man

Things other books don't tell you about men.

Onyx R. Linthicum, Jr.

ISBN: 978-0-578-12146-8

Table of Contents

The Cherry on Top
Things about men other books don't tell you.

Chapters

Acknowledgements

God is to be praised. I've been blessed to advise many personal friends about men, relationships and even marriage. Though I've never been married and have no formal training, life has been my training ground for such a time as this. God has a way of giving a person just what is needed, when it's needed. Much of the advice that I've given over the years has been from the testimonies of others whom I know personally. Here are excerpts I've compiled from multiple conversations and now share with you to make a difference in your lives and relationships. Each of the conversations I've had and every precious moment shared has had a significant impact on my life. Our paths crossed for this moment. Some will read and find their situations buried in the text. Know that blessings will follow your reading and you will find strength to endure your individual situations. I'm believing God to work in a mighty way through this writing. Be blessed.

Dedication

This book and the knowledge herein are dedicated to the strong women who possess it. I pray that the wisdom in this book and the Holy Spirit will help you discern those that present themselves to you. I pray that you will see past the mask, hear past the short talk and that their heart will be revealed to you. I pray that you will come into the knowledge of who they are in Christ Jesus and even more so, who you are in Christ Jesus as you expect God's very best to manifest in your life.

Introduction

Some may wonder why I titled the book the way I did and it's a valid question. It's simple. Regardless of his ethnicity, he's still a man. Now I get that there are cultural differences but he's still a man. He may be wealthy or he may be poor but yes you got it, he's still a man. I conceived the idea to write it from discussions with friends and listeners of my online radio show, Peer Talk (www.Peer-Talk.com). Many had read numerous help guides on understanding men but much of what they were reading was outdated, as I discovered from reading some of the same publications. It frustrated me to the point of wanting to really talk about what I know so well – how men think. For those who read some of the other stuff, I hope it was helpful. Let's say you got your ice cream and whipped cream and maybe even a few bananas. Should we even mention the nuts you've come across? No pun intended. It's now time to top all of that stuff off and what better topping than the infamous cherry.

Now I'm giving it to you raw and right because I've been the player and I've been played. I've said the things they wanted to hear and heard only what I chose to hear. Though a man doesn't really consciously think about it at the time it's taking place, and few will admit it: I've used women and have been used by them. Nothing in this book is new to me so I'm speaking from first-hand knowledge. I'm not bragging or boasting about it and I don't take it lightly. It's by the grace of the living God that I'm here to tell you what I've come to know. I'm not ashamed to admit my shortcomings and realize that what I've been through is what makes me want to do this all the more. In fact, I'm proud of my testimony because I know that God will use it for someone else's good. Some will read and shake their heads in disbelief, refusing to acknowledge that it's themselves they see in this mirror. Others will see themselves and realize they need to change. And then there will be those who will identify with the text because they're either going through or are just coming out of a situation they're reading about. I don't expect everyone to agree with my perspective and only ask that you allow what will to penetrate the areas of your life that need it most then share what you learn.

1

He Knows You Will Call

After he put in work and left you tongue tied and sucking on your thumb, guess what? He knows you'll call - again. Why do I say this? You just met the lover of your life. No I didn't say the "love" of your life, but "lover." He was better than the last, who was better than the last, etc., etc. If you're reading this and understand the hidden innuendos in the first sentence of this paragraph, you know what I mean. You're probably not a virgin and have had a few of these encounters. As we navigate through our sexcapades in life, we often hit points where we stop ourselves and ask, "What the hell am I doing?" It's in those moments that we believe we want and deserve more than wild, passionate nights of lust. You may be asking, "Who would ask such a thing?" However, many will admit that those moments of finite pleasure are far and few between and get old. Afterwards we have to deal with the emptiness and loneliness that are left behind when the other party has grabbed their things and headed out of the door. We then make a commitment to ourselves to "stop it!" and embark on a path to do what we perceive as the right thing. Of course this means something different to everyone but for many, including myself, it's an effort to really focus on enjoying being single, celibate and developing a stronger relationship with God. Our budgeting improves as does our work ethic and we actually begin to complete projects we started that fell to the way side when "he or she" became THE significant part of our lives. We believe that by doing these things, we are preparing ourselves for that lasting relationship with our soul mate when he or she shows up. This often fruitless attempt lasts for a period of time and then it's back to the norm and guess what? We're on the phone making those booty calls all over again and watching our lives come unraveled again. I know I'm not by myself. In fact you may be saying, "Damn. He just called me out". It's ok, we're in this together. The important part of it all is to recognize what you're doing wrong so you can make the necessary changes – which we admittedly do. However the bigger piece of this puzzle is to understand what you have to do to maintain your course of action and not revert. In other words, if you want change, you have to change. Understand your purpose for making the change. What are the pros and cons? What sacrifices are you willing to make to obtain that peace that passes all understanding? Are you willing to say "No" when he calls you to come over? Or better still, are you willing to say "No" I refuse to make that call because I deserve more?"

Scenario #1. You've dated this person for 6 months but you started sleeping together in 2 weeks. Big deal.

Side note: Where did that term come from? Half the time people aren't spending the night afterwards so nobody is sleeping together. We just had sex and now one of us is going home. Okay back to the scenario.

He's an ok guy and you're digging him and he's digging you - or so you're led to believe. The lovemaking is on point but that's about it. He has the gift for gab but you're not going out and spending any real quality time. You've settled because he makes you climb the headboard. You've replaced more ripped sheets than you can count from clutching them too hard and your nail tech and stylist are on speed dial. Still something is missing in the form of quality time and you've raised this point on a number of occasions only to receive the typical response: "I've just been busy and I'm trying to see you as much as I can (which is normally late at night just before bed time). After a period of time you become fed up and you start to argue more about your unfulfilling relationship with him. You express it to some of your confidants and they advise you to leave. Some more time passes and one night after yet another broken promise to get together earlier that evening, he shows up late around bed time of course and you find yourself, once again, engaging in another meaningless, unfulfilling, sexual encounter. The next day, you express to him that you don't want to do this anymore. He attempts to justify his actions but you're not hearing it. Nonetheless, he leaves with an attitude. You, on the other hand, are too upset, frustrated and downright aggravated to shed a tear. "What a loser," you think to yourself of him and you vow to cut him off.

Here's where the problem comes in. Upon his exit he's already thinking, "She'll call me when she cools off." And not a good two weeks later, sure enough, you're on the phone with him discussing what happened and how you can fix it and move forward - together. Here's what many fail to understand. He's not going to change. You just think he will. He knows and has been anticipating this weak moment since he left and knew that when your hormones got the best of you, you'd be calling and now he's on his way over to give you that temporary fix you called him for. That's right, you thought you were calling him to discuss getting back together but the truth is, if you're honest with yourself, you wanted some and you wanted him to give it to you. He "did" you right and he's the one you want and are willing to tolerate until the next Mr. Right comes along and "does" you better. This is the unspoken truth in many relationships.

You're probably asking "Well, how can the next Mr. Right come along if I'm focused on my man?" It's really quite simple. He'll be the one you meet at a party or the new guy at work even. He's full of great conversation and is very easy to talk to. He appears to be a confidant and someone you can share those secrets of your relationship with. Oh and one of the most important things is - he makes you laugh. Ahhhh!!! How refreshing is that? By now you've forgotten what laughter is so he's a breath of fresh air, and he's easy on the eyes. That's a bonus. Okay ready for another scenario?

Scenario #2: It starts with the occasional lunch date but you don't call it that. You're just grabbing a bite, right? Yeah ok. He's in your corner and seems to dislike what's going on between you and your man just as much as you do. He's your knight is shining armor who seems to whisk you away like Calgon when you need that break. Your casual lunch encounters spill over into texting into the late evening hours. He wants to call you but he maintains distance in lieu of your current situation. Wouldn't want to raise any eyebrows or red flags now would you? Believe it or not he still respects the other man but he's not going to miss his opportunity either. The texting soon becomes more aggressive flirtation that leads to sexting. Okay for those of you who don't quite understand that term let me enlighten you. Sex by text. How's that? These exchanges often speak of sexual encounters and often involve the exchange of provocative photographs. So much for the imagination right? Now it's right there in color on that television sized screen for a cell phone. Soon you're comfy enough with those exchanges that videos follow. Eventually this virtual pleasure along with those occasional lunches and periodic phone calls throughout the day make you forget about the messy relationship you're dealing with. As a reader, you've probably forgotten about her man so let's bring him back into the picture now.

In many cases, none of this has gotten past him. He realizes that you're not fussing and cussing at him as much. He also realizes that the conversations and your pokes at spending more time with him have diminished. Now the flags are being raised. Pay attention to the next part ladies (and gentlemen) because this may be your chance to escape free and clear of the drama. This is applicable to men as well because it really does happen both ways. However, for the sake of consistency we'll continue the scenario. Watch this. Because the flags are raised and he sees the handwriting on the wall. He is going to do one of two things: assume, then ask "What's up?" Prepare yourself for this conversation because there's no way to avoid it. It's best to have it and get it over with. You have one choice but two options. You will choose to answer because you have to. He won't let you not answer and you'll make yourself guilty by default if you don't. However the options are to tell the truth or lie. If in your mind this relationship is over you may as well tell the truth, hurt his ego and move on. However, if you don't believe it's over and you are planning to hold onto your "playette" card, you'll lie and think of some farfetched reason for communicating so frequently with this other man. Careful with this option though. You've been given an out that doesn't come too often. Now you have to assess whether the new guy is going to replace the old guy or if he's going to remain your occasional confidant or lunch time buddy. At this point it's likely that you haven't slept with him and makes the decision a little more difficult because what if he's a dud in bed, hmmmm? You'll be calling your ex again. Exactly. Oh, but by then it may be too late. Now you're stuck. Even worse, what if the new guy turns out to be a bigger jerk after you've become intimate?

These are those defining moments we get to in life where we have to decide what is most important to a healthy relationship? Is all I need a stud in bed or do I need someone I can communicate with, who values and cherishes me beyond the bedroom door? Ask many and few will tell you they've found both. Ultimately, many have become content in their situations and have tricked themselves to believe that the real extent of love is what they are already getting. How many experience true love at its best?

2

He Waits for Two Reasons

Think about something for a moment. After doing it the wrong way for so long you've decided that your goodies are way too valuable to just continue to share like a smorgasbord with every man that crosses your path and pays you a compliment. You've read a couple of relationship books that tell you that you should wait and so you decide to do just that. You're going to hold out and make him sweat a bit until you feel a little more certain of his motive. You want to know that it's you he's interested in and not your body or money. Yes, men will go after money as well. The sky's the limit if he's "putting it down right." However, you're a little smarter than that so you begin your quest of celibacy. Sure enough after an extended period of about a week (yes, I said a week) you meet Mr.

Right now. He smells good, he looks good and you can't wait to see how good he tastes (keep your mind focused). I'm referring to his lips. After all, you're keeping it above the waistline for now. He's got the gift for gab and guess what? He has professed that he wants to wait before getting physical with you. Whoaaaa!!! He said it before you did. He's got to be a keeper.

Time goes on and you date for a couple of weeks. You've been seeing each other daily and from what you can tell, nothing's changed. He's still the same guy you met a few weeks earlier. He's showing consistency and this is something new for you. Well, now you're faced with a decision. You've heard of the 90day rule but is that really necessary? You want to wait and so does he - or so he says. In fact, you haven't even discussed sex in any way. You've spent the time getting to know each other. One evening after a great date of dining and dancing you decide to give in. You invite him in and it's on. I'll skip the juicy details since this isn't the book for that. But go back to the first sentence of the book and you'll get the idea. Sure enough, when he's done, he grabs his things and he's out the door. You sleep like a baby anticipating the usual morning call to discuss plans for the day. The phone doesn't ring. Concerned for his safety and to be sure he made it home alright you pick up the phone and make the call. He doesn't answer. Your concern increases as the day goes by and after several failed attempts to reach him. Finally, he answers with some lame excuse that you reluctantly accept. You're just glad he's ok. Keep in mind you're only weeks into this relationship. As the days go by the phone calls become increasingly far and few between and you wonder what is going on. Everything was great before you gave in so what is the problem. Your first notion is to assume the blame. Was it good enough? Did you please him? Was he satisfied? The blame soon turns to concern: Is there another woman? Is he married? What follows next in many cases, is THE answer: Did he get what he wanted and is no longer interested? Or even more: Did he really want to get to know me?

Sorry folks, this is reality. Often times he'll hang out for as long as he has to in order to get what he wants. Best believe that if this is the case, he's not going without. There are others out there who aren't presenting the same challenge. He's getting it from somewhere. He is snacking so he's not going hungry. So why wait on you? I'm glad you ask. Perhaps you presented the biggest challenge. He's used to those who say 'yes' right off the cuff and he's already put them in a special category and labeled it "snacks." Since you are challenging him, you're building his hunger. Rather than snack off of you, he wants to take his time and savor you slowly. You're going to be the catch of THAT day. Since men are natural competitors the goal at the end of the day is to be able to say "I got the prize and you didn't." He even wants to show the prize off. So yeah people are aware of who you are. He doesn't try to hide you hence the going out and having a great time. You're now asking yourself the typical question: "How could I be so stupid to get played like this?" Okay. Don't look at it that way. Instead, take it as a lesson learned that all men wait for what they want. Your job is to hold out. Don't do this just to be selfish and conniving but rather to build as much certainty as you can to protect your own integrity. Hey, and don't be afraid to get what you need out of the situation along the way. There are lots of nice restaurants to be tried. Certainly you're worth a great meal from time to time. **I caution that this isn't about using anybody and I don't advocate that at all.** However, if he's going to eventually "get it," then at least be sure he pays for it.

Now I have to flip the script. I sure hope my little scenarios are helpful in driving my points home. Let's take the exact same scenario up through you giving in. Now let's say that not only does the anticipated call come in the morning to make plans for the day but he even sent you that courtesy text to let you know he made it home safely last night. This is great. Now you're thinking "he's considerate, he really cares and he's an animal in bed". Congratulations! Sounds like you've got yourself a winner. The perfect ending to this is that he is all those things and a lot more which you discover as you continue to get to know each other and eventually marry and live happily ever after. Unfortunately, the first scenario is where a lot of women (and men) find themselves. Let's look at why he (or she) will wait.

Simply put, there are really only two reasons to wait. You either get what you wanted and you can leave now or you've found what you're looking for and there's no need to look any further. Let's break them both down, shall we?

You got what you wanted:

This is pretty simple. When you go to the store to pick up a loaf of bread, that's what you do. You get the bread (and a few other snack items since you're there) and you go home. Real simple, right? After you've eaten, you're full and you leave the kitchen to tend to other things. You have those extra snacks to nibble on until you're ready for another big meal. Can you see where I'm going with this? Are you the big meal or are you the snack? Only you can determine what you're willing to be. Neither is a guarantee for finding love. It really is a gamble. I would venture to say that there are many who waited years for marriage before being sexually active with their spouse only to result in eventual divorce. They tried to do it the right way but after a while, one of them started humming a familiar B.B. King tune - The Thrill Is Gone. We can even look beyond sex. Perhaps the motive is money, inheritance, fame and prestige. Motives are different so the more you have to offer the more they have to gain. Therefore, there are way more questions you have to ask yourself AND that other person to help make a proper assessment of their motives.

You've found what you're looking for:

Anybody who's ever searched for something and had difficulty finding it knows the anxiety that goes along with the physical exertion required by such an effort. Think about it. Singles, you know the frustration of wanting to have that special someone in your life and continuously meeting the wrong one. Imagine losing the diamond from your wedding ring. You would tear the place apart to find that diamond. It's no different when searching for Mr. or Mrs. Right. Some wait almost a lifetime to find that one thus marrying at 60+ years old. It happens and there's nothing wrong with it. The point is, when you find it and know it, show it. That's the key of all keys. You have to recognize that this is what you've been looking for and take advantage of the opportunity to lock it down and put a protective order on it. You now need to let the world know that this belongs to you. Now it becomes ok to use the word "mine" that your parents and teachers taught you was selfish as a child. This is not something you want to share with anyone and you are now ready to profess this to the world.

If you really look at it, are there really any other reasons to wait other than selfish gain, sex or a real sincerity to want to love that other person? Best believe your situation is going to fall into one of those categories. If there is another, please enlighten me.

3

You'll Never Change His Mind

This is the one thing you'll never do. He's a man so he has ego, testosterone and attitude. Your stuff might be platinum but it is not more powerful than his sheer will to do what he chooses. Oh, you may finagle a fur and even a diamond ring. You may even get the title of fiancée but until he's ready to say I do, you won't. The common belief is that men are afraid when they are refusing to pop the question. Truthfully, can you blame us? With marriages going to hell in a hand basket left and right and having to deal with the complexities of divorce - who wants to risk it? "Things are great just the way they are." This is what he may be saying so why the rush to add the title of Mrs. to HIS last name?

Even the Bible says in Philippians 4:6:

> "Be anxious for nothing, but in everything by prayer and supplication with thanksgiving let your requests be made known to God."

Stop rushing. If God sent him and it's ordained by God to be, in time and when he's ready, he'll propose. Now you may be bitter because you've spent the last 5 years in this current relationship without a whisper of marriage. Now you're wondering if it will ever happen. Reality check: If you're in your twenties, there's still hope. Perhaps you both are searching for your career niche. There's a chance that you've graduated but really haven't established a foothold on life. These are valid reasons to wait. After all, how can a man lead if he hasn't the skills to do so? How can he provide unless he has the necessary resources? Why would you follow knowing this?

For my middle-aged, 40+ readers, there is still a glimmer of hope that even if you're in this situation, he may pop the question. However, it is less likely. Let me explain why. By this time, many men have tasted the bitter and sweet of that union. Unfortunately for many, it's a taste they can do without. Companionship is what they desire; a friend with benefits. On the flip side, there are other men willing to take a chance at love again so they throw their hat in the ring for another chance to fight for what they believe in - the sanctity of marriage. You'll be one of the fortunate ones to meet this man. In many cases he will come with no drama and bearing little if any luggage. He's older now and has fought through many of the challenges of life. He's come out on top and has proven his leadership ability. His kids, if any, are grown and independent. They respect him and his decisions so you will probably have no opposition from them as his new wife when that time comes. He's pretty easy going as life has not only hardened him in certain areas but has also made him more sensitive in others. However, don't get it twisted. He is far from being a pushover and believes in leading the way for his family, particularly those in his household. Life has taught him a lot and he's more alert than ever. It's very unlikely that much is going to get past him. He's still guarded and on alert, rightfully so, to protect his investment. He doesn't plan on going down that lonely road again. He got in the ring to fight for you and he'll stay there because he is a fighter. As the saying goes, "What doesn't kill you makes you stronger." He's stronger and it's going to take a lot to tear him from you. This being said, perhaps love is actually better the second time around. I don't know but I'm sure many can speak to this.

Now let's get back to why you'll never change his mind. Men are not complex. Even women admit this. However, we are stubborn and determined. Challenging our decisions, as slight as it may be, is indirectly challenging our manhood. This is a big no no and often leads to disagreements and misunderstandings. If you read nothing else in this book, read this and I'll put it in bold letters so you'll easily reference it later: ***Men don't like confrontation. We like peace.*** Real men don't wake up waging war. We are generally forced into battle and we do so with honor because we know what's at stake. Trust me when I tell you, you don't want a 24-hour warrior. You do want a man who is ready for battle to protect your honor.

The Bible says in James 1:19:

> "My dear brothers, take note of this: Everyone should be quick to listen, slow to speak and slow to become angry".

A man fired up on all cylinders, at all times is a force you don't want to have to deal with. Understanding the temperament of a man is also crucial to understanding how much he'll allow you to push. Pushing too much can cause him to run or provoke anger. It is unlikely it will result in a happy ending for you. If he runs then you've just forced him out the door because he wasn't ready. If he gets angry, you may want to reconsider how effectively he communicates and what it takes to push his buttons. If he is quick tempered, you may want to consider forcing him out the door because this could lead to major problems down the line if you decide to stick it out. Then there's one more possibility. I said you can't change his mind but there is a little exception to that rule. It is possible in some cases for him to have a moment of compassion and give in. This is dangerous for you because at that moment, he really wants to make you happy. This has been his mission all along – to see his baby smiling. However, it still doesn't mean he's ready for that "all in" commitment. In this moment of compassion he gives in and pops the question. He presents you with the most beautiful ring you've ever seen – yours. It may be the tiniest diamond ever and may be set in a sterling silver setting but it's yours and this is the moment that you've been waiting for. You say "yes" and jump on the phone and Facebook to tell the world. The questions pour in. "When is the big day?" they all ask. So when is it? Have you discussed it yet? That is the next big question even before you start subscribing to all the bridal magazines (if you haven't already).

The ring is on your hand and the word is in the streets but you still don't have a date in mind. By now, he's realized what he did. To him that was a "what have I done?" moment. It's too late now. He can't exactly ask you for the ring back and say "oops". Instead, as you begin trying to map out a date, he comes with the excuses. No time seems to be a good time. He says you should have more money saved up so you don't go into debt to pay for it. He wants to be sure his job is stable because he wants to be certain he can provide for his wife and family. All of these sound valid but honestly, they're excuses. The truth is, the day he asked should have been a great time. Realistically, how much does a marriage license cost? Last, his job status should be stable before he even asks you so why is job stability an issue now? He isn't ready. He simply wanted to shut you up. I'm just telling it like it is. You forced him to do something he really wasn't ready to do and now you're going to have to call all those people back and explain this to everybody on Facebook. You jumped the gun and there isn't going to be a wedding, at least not right now.

Now let me help you understand how to know when a man is ready. He'll ask you. That's it. There's nothing complex about it and no explanation is necessary. When he's ready you'll know because he will let you know without pressure, that he is ready. Nagging him and throwing hints are not going to win him over. I often have this conversation with women and I always say the same thing. It's ok to have discussions about marriage and to even let your intentions and desires be known. At least this way it's out there. The important thing is not to give him the impression that you are trying to rush him down the aisle. Pay attention to what he tells you in his reply to your candid profession.

4

Listen – He's Telling the Truth

It's obvious that men and women do not communicate the same way. Our forms of communication are light years away from each other but we say the same things and desire the same results. It's as if we're speaking in other tongues that require interpretation. At the end of the day, we all want to love and be loved. How do we get to that point? Even this is simple. We learn about each other. I learn what makes you move and you learn what makes me move. I learn what ticks you off and you do the same. Forget the fact that we're male and female. Even this difference, though relevant, doesn't overshadow the fact that we are humans who are individual and full of emotions.. What moves me may not be the same as anyone you may come in contact with but you won't know this unless you take the time to find out. It is imperative, particularly in the early stages of getting to know someone, that you listen. At this stage of the game, no one typically has anything to lose so while he can lie, why would he? Yes, we often send representatives to the table but again, if you're doing due diligence and assessing properly, you are comparing his words to his actions to see if they are lining up. If you find too many inconsistencies, it's a good possibility that he's not who he is trying to appear to be. Bail now!! Don't get caught up in a tangle of lies and deceit. If you stick around you'll become so mixed up in his web of deceit that you'll start making excuses for him. You deserve better than that. If people put their cards on the table up front then it gives others a fair opportunity to assess the extent of damage they may have to repair if they're going to pursue more.

"He said he loved me". Yes he did and he meant every word of it. Consider yourself fortunate. Ladies, understand that these are not meaningless words to men. In fact, it may take a very long time for some men to use them in the first place. You wait and continue waiting to hear them and they never come from his lips to your ears. This is because we know that you take these words very seriously and if we're going to use them, a ring is sure to follow not long after or it should. Now this is also dependent on the type of relationship and love we're referring to. Do I love you like a brother or sister? Am I professing to be in love with you or is it really just lust? All of these are communication points. Both parties should understand completely the type of love being exchanged in order to be clear about motives. If you're not clear, ask. There's nothing wrong with asking what you don't know. Don't assume. It can come back and bite you on your butt later. Later in the book, I'm going to help you with certain questions and instruct you on how to ask them so that you don't appear to be nagging. There really is a strategy to getting answers to those all important questions.

Understand when asking questions that it is a two way communication. One person is asking the questions and the other person is answering them. You both will get an opportunity. Keep in mind that this is not a rush job. People spend huge durations of their adult lives learning about one another and they still never completely do. A lot of the fun is in asking the questions and getting the answers. Just when you think you know someone, here comes another question you have to ask. Make a game out of it. People are naturally inquisitive and have a desire to know. As the questions are given, answers will result. When asking the questions, be sure not to ask questions you really fear the answers to. "You can't handle the truth" is a true statement. But only you know if you can or not. More importantly, if you're going to ask, you must be mature enough to handle the answers in a civil way. You may have to wait to ask certain questions until you have reasoned with yourself enough. What you don't want is to cause that confrontation that we discussed earlier and scare him off from answering any further questions. How you handle his answers will determine his comfort level in answering them. If you fly off the handle to even one of his answers, you may as well close up the shop and hang the "going out of business" sign on the door. He WILL become a recluse and your chances of getting answers in the future are going to be challenging to say the least.

If you're successful at asking the right questions, you will get great answers. If you're successful at handling the answers, you stand the chance of cultivating a very open and honest relationship. You may ask how you can handle certain answers with grace and refrain from choking the life out of him or her. One important thing to remember is that they are not sharing these often personal details with you to be judged. They're sharing to give you some insight into their past or their present. Don't beat them up about it but rather consider this a privilege that they've allowed you into their world for these brief moments. It's an opportunity that perhaps few have been granted. It's like an exclusive. You don't want to shoot your chances down of getting another one so play your cards right and be nice and understanding.

Why do men lie is a question women always ask. Well why do women lie? Is either really necessary? Let's go one more and ask why do people lie? I'm not going to sit here and answer this from a scientific perspective: that there are chemicals in the brain that mix with other chemicals thus causing a chemical reaction that causes someone to utter a lie. No, that's way too deep. The bottom line response to this question, less scientific and more social, is simple: they choose to. The real question now is why do they choose to? Fear of... (you fill in the blanks). As a child, when you broke your mother's antique vase and chose to say "I didn't do it," you lied. You lied to keep from getting your "tail tore up." So fear is what kept you from telling the truth. There are countless incidents you can probably recall for telling a tale as my momma used to call them. We weren't allowed to say "lie". It was a bad word in the house and could cost you a few teeth. So when you ask why a person chooses to lie, only he/she can answer that question. You can only make a reasonable assumption.

It can be confusing sometimes because what sounds like the truth could be a lie and what sounds like a lie could also be the truth. Don't assume. It's very important to listen and try a person by their actions. Again, this is something the Bible is very clear on in the book of John. Hear what they say and watch what they do. Faith without works is dead. So if their mouth is not lining up with their actions, there's a good chance that there's a bit more to this person than meets the eye.

5

The Big "No-No" Rule

It's been said that one of the biggest deal breakers of any friendship is dating a friend's ex. I've had friends who have confirmed to me that there is no way they could. Why is this? I've asked this question over and over again and I get the same answer. It's an unwritten rule that friends live by. To date a friend's ex is breaking that rule and you are subject to being denounced as a friend and ridiculed by peers. Unbelievable!!! Why on earth should you even care what an ex is doing and with whom? Is it not true that people change? Just because things didn't work out between you and the other person doesn't mean that they won't for someone else, including a friend. I've heard stories of connects that happen years, and I do mean twenty plus years later, between ex's and friends that result in the destruction of life-long friendships. Excuse me, but if you dated him 20 years ago and you're now married to someone else, why on earth would you care that a good friend connects with him those same 20 years later? I'll tell you why. It's your selfishness and ego.

You're afraid of the man he's become. You're afraid that she's going to have what you didn't – a wonderful experience with a man who wasn't ready to love you the same way at that time. I would venture to say that you could also be afraid of being compared to her, particularly in the areas of lovemaking. Either way, the thought of seeing the two of them together is just something you cannot bear. Their happiness together is something you can't deal with although you're already in a blissful marriage. Again I ask why should you care? Selfish is what it is. You are ultimately blocking their blessing to spare your selfish ego. You may even argue that he was trifling way back then and you don't want her to go through the emotional heartache you endured. This assumes that he hasn't changed over the years. Perhaps the same or similar life experiences that have shaped you as a woman all these years have had no impact on him. He has to be the same boy you knew back then and he means your friend no good at all. Forget the fact that he's been through his own relationship ups and downs, perhaps a divorce for which she was at fault. Let's not consider that he's now a responsible single father raising a son and daughter by himself. You used to foot the bill so there's no way he has a successful career and can afford some of the finer tastes in life on occasion. Forget that he spends much of his time mentoring others and making a difference in their lives. In your mind he is the same guy that you broke up with years ago. You really don't care if he falls in love - just not with someone you know. Should they not have a fair shot at the same love you're experiencing and if they can provide that to one another, you as a friend should be a staunch supporter.

There is an exception to this rule in my book, however. Though I may be referred to as an opportunist, even I have boundaries. Personally, I draw the line at marrying a friend's ex or even worse, a loved one's ex. Perhaps the latter could even be considered incest. Either way, once the ring has been given and that covenant established, he or she is off the market permanently in my book. I'm speaking for self so if this doesn't necessarily make you cringe then have at it. I just look at marriage and platonic relationships in a whole different light. Platonic relationships certainly have rules and boundaries but there is no letter of commitment here that says I'm obligated to you in any way. I don't have to pay your bills, take care of you when you're sick, serve up sex. Nor am I really obligated or responsible to or for you in any way. I just choose to acknowledge you as the person I have selected for this indefinite period of time. Either of us can pack up and walk at any time with no questions asked. Well there will probably be many questions flying but I'm referencing a perfect world scenario. I know it sounds cold but it is reality.

Marriage adds a different dimension though. When married, all of those obligations become rules of doing business with no exceptions. That business is the compromises and negotiations you agree to that make your marriage strong. You WILL provide for, take care of, serve sex to and are otherwise obligated to be sure that nobody else is doing these things for your significant other. If you don't handle your business, rest assured that another business partner will do it for you. If someone else is handling these bulleted items then you've got a much bigger problem on your hands and your marriage is doomed. Prepare to close up shop. Therefore, my reason for feeling strongly about not coming second to a marriage is probably more spiritual than personal. That covenant regardless of separation or divorce, in my opinion, is one that will always remain. I just choose not to be a part of a covenant that remains between two of my friends.

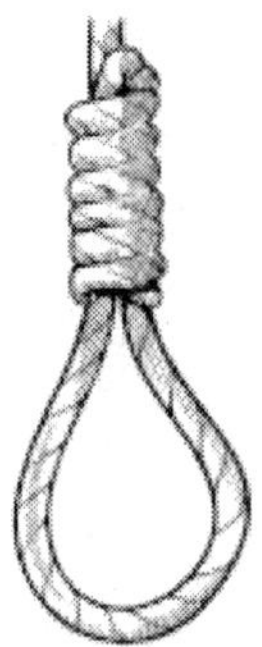

6

I'll Never Tell How I Found Out - Here's the Rope

I'm a middle aged man who has had several relationships, flings, one-night stands, booty calls and many other terms that you may have heard or perhaps not. At any rate I've had my share of acquaintances of many sorts. I've certainly felt the sting of heartbreak and experienced unreciprocated love. I've hurt and been hurt. I've stepped on and been stepped on. I've had the misfortune of being turned down by women I would have married and the frustration of being pursued by those I would have never considered. I've allowed my lustful nature to consume time in my life that I will never regain. Looking back, this time could have been used so much more productively and to a greater benefit for me and others. These are the things that have shaped me, created apprehension and groomed me for the day I say "I do."

Though some might say these are moments to regret, I don't. They are the life lessons that I can speak of like no other because they are exclusive to me. These are my moments of testimony that I can share with my kids and adult peers that may prevent them from making the same mistakes. Perhaps you have your own. Don't frown about them but instead thank God that he got you through them. Now it's your obligation to share them with others and not be ashamed of them. Perhaps you have a book in you now. Write it! Now before I go way beyond my reason for this chapter, I will get back to the title and share with you why I'll never tell how I found out.

Found out what? I'm glad you asked. Throughout my escapades in relationships I've always been an analytical person. I simply hate to argue. Debate yes, argue no. There's nothing like a good debate to get the blood flowing. I'll debate with those I know I'll lose against just to get their feathers ruffled and then I'll bow out gracefully, leaving them heated as I chuckle and walk away. It's all in fun. However, in relationships I watch and listen. I do what I told you to do earlier in the book. I compare actions to words and when they don't line up I pay attention. This is the handwriting on the wall. If something becomes inconsistent there's probably more to it than meets the eye. Don't ignore it. You have to investigate, ask questions and do your own assessment. You have to do these things to establish your own comfort level. If you're more passive and something is going on that you don't know about, you run the risk of being trampled and hurt really badly. Now some can be compulsive about this by being on constant guard. Hurt from the past can cause you to be extremely guarded. You MUST give your significant other a margin for error but also the benefit of the doubt that he or she will do right by you. You can't choke the life out of the relationship by putting a noose around it from the start.

I like to say it this way: **I'm going to hand you the rope when I ask you questions. How you respond tells me what you chose to do with the rope. You can lie to me (hang yourself) or you can tell the truth and retain my respect for at least being honest, which may make it easier for me to trust you and establish communication to fix the problem.**

Some jump the gun and begin asking questions right away when they sense a problem. I'm not saying this is wrong. I'm not a relationship therapist. I just know what works for me. Since I've always been the analytical type, I typically won't confront anyone with a problem until I'm 99.9% sure that there really is one. By this time I normally have the proof I need and the case is made. That's when I hand over the rope. You may be thinking that's not fair to the other person but keep in mind I haven't acted on the problem. I'm just in protection mode so I'm not real concerned about their feelings right now. I'm trying to protect mine. I'm simply establishing whether there is a problem and the best way to act on it. By the time I do, I already know and have proof. You see cheaters make every effort to cover their tracks but if you're lucky, you'll have a cheater who's not very good at it and you'll uncover them. How you do this is up to you but there are many ways and some don't cost a penny and don't require you to be a 007. Use your imagination and I'm sure you will come up with several ways. That's as much as I will say about that. Don't get mad because I didn't spell out my tactics. You have to get your own. The media does enough to tell the bad guys how the good guys found them out. The bad guys need to be caught making the same stupid mistakes so I'll continue to let them and you should too. Don't tell.

7

No Question is Off Limits

I think we all agree that communication is the key to successful relationships of any sort. If we can't, there is nothing we can do together. Effective communication allows us to move cohesively. It allows us to determine if we're on the same page or if we're even moving in the right direction. This isn't to say that we must agree on everything but we have to be able to recognize that we don't and what compromises need to be made if necessary. We have to be able to discuss everything and I do mean EVERYTHING. No question is off limits when you're getting to know someone. Honesty is crucial. The person is asking because they want to know. Here's your opportunity to be up front. Though they may not need to know at this time, their curiosity is peaked. You can respectfully decline an answer with an explanation or you can answer it and get it out of the way. If you decline, best believe the question isn't avoided but it will peak their curiosity even more. They'll now want to know what the big secret is all about. By putting it all out there, you can each decide if this is someone you really want to spend the time getting to know. It works both ways to both your benefits.

Ladies, there are certain questions you should avoid asking in the very beginning. There are questions that can make men run if they are not tactful and asked at the right time. Now I'm going to get into that list of questions I mentioned earlier. I find it hard to discuss me. I don't have a problem talking about my interests. In doing so, it often offers insight into me. By getting to know my interests you can get a pretty good gauge of the kind of person I am. This is all a part of the listening process that we talked about in the earlier chapter: Listen–He's Telling the Truth.

I had the opportunity to interview a number of business owners for a literary piece I was working on many years ago. Prior to each interview I prepared a question list to use as a guide for our conversation. What I discovered is that by asking a mixture of questions including open-ended and pointed questions, I was able to do more listening than talking. Often, as I asked the first of several questions, all I had to do was sit back and check off the other questions as they were speaking. It was in conducting these interviews that I discovered how much people enjoy discussing their interests and the things they enjoy. For these people, their business was their main passion and they found it very easy and comfortable to discuss it. Though I asked questions about their family and other more personal questions, somehow they always ended up back at the business or those things they were most passionate about.

People enjoy discussing things. Those who prefer to discuss self are often referred to as arrogant or conceited. I won't go that far to say this. Instead I'll give them the benefit of the doubt and say that perhaps they're just more comfortable discussing themselves than others. This said, ladies and gents in the beginning it may be a good idea to limit conversations to personal interests. These questions allow you to determine any commonalities and help direct further conversations. I also don't advocate coming up with a checklist of questions as I did for the interviews. This may make you look a little silly and desperate. Instead, use open-ended questions and let it flow. Play off the responses you get. This is not speed dating so you don't have to switch to rapid fire mode and begin firing off questions. Take time to digest the answers you get, laugh and just enjoy the moment. One answer can spark 5 additional questions. The key is to listen carefully and speak less. Remember this if you don't remember anything else you read in this book: he wants to impress you as much as you want to impress him. Be as candid as you can when it's your turn. Don't just answer his questions but give him something to work with that will make him ask for more.

One of the worst things in the world and a quick way to know a conversation may be null is when a person says "tell me something about you." This isn't a formal interview and shouldn't be treated as such. Their response is probably going to be, "What do you want to know?" Cut to the chase and just ask what you want to know. Again, remember to use open-ended questions. Here is where you'll get the biggest bang for your buck. If you ask what is your favorite color you will get a one word answer and nothing more. Instead, if you must ask that question ask it this way: "Tell me your favorite color and why it is so significant." Ahhh!! Now you're going to get some intellectual answers. He may say his favorite color is purple like mine but now you'll find out that he likes that color because it is symbolic of royalty. Now you're thinking "is he a king or a prince?" Probably not but he may think highly of himself and hold himself to higher standards. I don't mean this in a bad way. Now you've learned more than his favorite color. You've actually learned how he feels about himself and perhaps those he associates himself with. This is a mere example but I think you get the point. Try it!

You now understand how discussions about interests can create hours of inquisitive fun.

Learning about each other is really a fun thing to do but it takes time and understanding. Some questions will be more difficult to answer and even ask and some will be just downright uncomfortable. These are hurdles that you can help one another overcome. As I said much earlier on, it's important not to judge. Don't show disgust or extreme surprise in the answers you get. Discuss them and get an understanding behind them. Here you'll learn successes and things that may not have gone quite right in their lives. Further discussion will help you know whether they learned from the experience or are subject to repeat it. How will you be impacted either way?

Along with ok questions there are the not-so-ok questions that you should be aware of. These include initial questions about marriage, sex, money and children. These questions are best reserved for later discussion after the preliminary questions have been answered and you've gotten past first base. This just means after you've established a comfort level with this person and have gotten over the comfort hurdles we mentioned. If you determine this person will be nothing more than a good friend, then the not-so- ok questions don't need to be discussed in the first place. You have to put people in a category and leave them there. Don't mix your categories. It will become confusing and a big headache. This is when you get into leading folks on. Are they a friend or a lover? Are they a lover or potential spouse? Identify these, categorize them and stick with it. I must admit that I've been guilty of doing this and it's a pain in the buttocks to deal with because you're constantly defending yourself and having discussions with those same individuals. Don't do it!!

8

What's Too Soon?

I'm glad you asked this question. However, the answer depends on what you're actually referring to.

- Too soon to call
- Too soon to go out
- Too soon to be serious
- Too soon to have sex

There are many "too soons" that you can apply this question to, but for the sake of time we will limit ours to these four questions. When is it too soon to call? If a number was given then there is no such thing as too soon. He gave you his number to call him. Why wait a week, a month or even longer to use it? Do you really expect him to remember who you are if you wait so long? I've had this to happen to me. I typically don't ask anyone for their number. I generally give mine and figure if there's a mutual interest, she'll use it. On the rare occasion that I do ask, I use it within a day or two. There are those exceptions where I have a busy schedule and end up waiting a bit longer and certainly run the risk of having to explain who I am when I finally call. There's something frustrating about having to explain who you are and where you met because you waited so long. Nobody likes to but if it's necessary, just do it. You did it to yourself so suck it up and pray the interest is still there. There's no need to get your drawers in a bunch. You may even have to send a photograph to refresh their memory so have a nice one ready to send. Next time you'll think twice about waiting so long.

When is too soon to go out? Well this is relative to your comfort level with this person. Perhaps you've known them for a while and just started communicating on this level so going out isn't a big deal. However, if you've just met it may take you a little longer to warm up and become comfortable enough to go out. Either way, remember this first date may determine if there will be another so represent well. This doesn't mean bring your representative but it does mean to allow your date to get to know you. If they don't like the real you on this date, then they will not like the real you down the line so don't waste your time trying to be who you aren't. Remember the conversation points we discussed earlier and just have fun with it. It's just a date. I'm sure he doesn't have a ring in his pocket to present to you this early in the game. If he does, RUN!! It's way too soon to even have discussions about marriage.

Okay the date went well and you're both feeling each other's vibe. So after a few dates is when you may want to explore taking things to the next level. This would be the exclusivity level. If you're ready to make that commitment to be serious, now's the time. I generally don't recommend making this decision too quickly. You may be asking how long it should take to make this commitment. The answer is it takes as long as it takes. There's no rush. You can take your time and be as sure as you feel you need to be. Don't allow anybody to pressure you into making this decision. It's all about comfort level – yours. This is the time to enjoy the ride and to stop and smell the roses along the way. You may not have even become intimate yet. Good!!! That's even better because right now all you have is the emotional attachment from spending time. Everybody knows that throwing sex into the mix is where the game changes along with every emotion a woman has. It's no secret that guys handle this part of a relationship totally different than women. For us, it's a physical act and nothing more. For women, it's the unspoken commitment without the ring.

That takes me to the next "too soon." When is it too soon for sex? Nobody can answer this question for you. Only you are in touch with your emotions and your passions. People can only suggest that you wait and that's not a bad idea no matter how you look at it. What are the cons of waiting? Are your loins going to explode if you don't get that release? Are you going to be the most evil person in the world because you're backed up? Is the world going to end and Jesus returns before you marry and can get it in? Well the last two are possibilities. I've seen attitude when folks are backed up and there is always the possibility of Jesus returning but the first one is a bit farfetched. I've never heard instances of this so you're probably pretty safe.

Waiting is a good thing because it gives the two people a chance to get to know other aspects of one another. They learn each other's interests and history. They find common likes and dislikes and discover new things together outside of the bedroom. Once sex is introduced a clear day can become hazy. Suddenly your thoughts become more driven to intimacy rather than just spending quality time. Moments away from this person can lead to insecurity as you wonder if they're being intimate with someone else. Notice how conversations always dive deep from general "How was your day, I missed you" to "Wow, you're a great lover and I can't wait to do it again". You've just cheapened the relationship because you jumped the gun. So when is the right time?

The Bible says in Hebrews 13:4:

> "Let marriage be kept honorable in every way, and the marriage bed undefiled. For God will judge those who commit sexual sins, especially those who commit adultery."

So the answer to believers is when you're married. Let's be realistic about this only from the perspective that we all know that few wait. If you're not going to take the spiritual answer then the next best answer would be simply when you're comfortable enough to realize that you are about to give the very best you have to this other person. If you're going to do this, at least recognize what you are going to get in return - if anything at all. Will you be another notch in their belt or will you become their prized possession? Whatever the answer and whatever the result, you will have to live with it. The important thing is to recognize that the best you have is you. How valuable are you to self to give yourself to another who may not value you the same way? Here is where most men and women fall short. They don't assess their own value. Sex has become the method of payment for "showing me a great evening". What is your worth? Does giving the best of you to someone equate to payment for a $65.00 dinner and a couple of glasses of cheap wine? So he picked you up in his S-class. So he's the finest man on earth in your eyes. Nobody said the devil doesn't send his very best to tempt God's very best. It's something to think about.

9

Games vs. Miscommunication

"Quit playin' game!" How many times have you heard that one? I've heard it numerous times and most importantly in those times that I really wasn't. Since the beginning of time there's been a degree of separation between men and women in the area of communication. Most often it's the woman who complains that he doesn't communicate. Though not unheard of, it's rare that the man complains about communication problems. Truth is men don't mind listening but we don't like to talk. In our minds silence is golden. If she isn't bitchin' and moaning then everything is A-OK. We communicate in our own way just not the way most women would prefer. It's got to be chemical because every man is wired this way. The person who writes the book and accurately deciphers the male communication code will instantly become a gazillionaire. There are numerous books that talk about communication but a bulleted cheat sheet on "what it means when he does this" would win the favor of all women. Understanding how a person thinks is key to effective communication. Since we don't all think alike, communication must be tailored to the individual. What moves my mountains won't necessarily move his and vice versa. What may be motivation to one person may have the opposite effect on someone else. Reverse psychology works on some but not all. With this in mind, it takes time to learn a person and their ways.

Getting to know someone isn't always a verbal act. I prefer to observe more than question. As the saying goes "actions speak louder than words" and if you pay attention, they sometimes scream "Run!" Take heed because words are just that until some action is applied. Watch the action and it will speak volumes about character and integrity. Don't ignore or brush off the obvious. As I mentioned earlier, it's important to listen because often times he's telling the truth even when he may appear to be joking. You can validate his words if you pay close attention to his actions. Though women often complain that men don't communicate, I don't think it's that. I believe it's more a matter of how we communicate and not understanding our methods. Just know that men don't like confrontation and that should be the warning to not approach us with intimidation, threats and attitude. You will always win him over with kindness. Anything else is going to create a problem as we become defensive, shutdown and retreat - that crawl into our shell and hide for a while until we're ready to discuss it, period.

Until we're ready to discuss it? Yes ladies, understand again as I drive home the earlier point about changing his mind. You can't. Men are peaceful by nature, competitive and determined. We don't like confrontation but thrive on competition.

Side note: You shouldn't be too loose with the cookies. Making it easy for us doesn't present a challenge and we WILL enjoy the moment but get bored quickly. Refrain and abstain is the name of the game. Yes, I'm a rapper so stay tuned for that project.

Ladies, you love to talk and we understand this. That's why God programmed us to listen more than we speak. This is one of the first things you should understand about a man. If you get this point, everything else will fall into place. Since we are better listeners, we are very analytical. It may take us hours to digest and dissect what you just said so don't expect a reply right away. We need time to pick apart what you said, analyze it and think about how to respond. This is why we sometimes have to have a follow up discussion later. Attempting to force our hand for an answer right now could be disastrous. Give him the time he needs. This is especially true during those heated moments of disagreement. Let him cool off. He's not going to forget the conversation but he does need time to ponder what was said and how to respond in a way that makes sense, doesn't provoke additional anger and provides a solution. That's another thing about us, we like to solve problems. There's something about it that makes us feel needed. Knowing we were able to save the day gives us a rush that is unexplainable and we will wear it as a badge for the world to know. Here's a moment to honor your man and show him he's the greatest. Build him up. Your doing this for him will only intensify his desire to show you all the more that he's the man.

One trait of a man is his determination. When he sets off on a mission, whether it's pursuit of a woman or any goal he sets for himself, he's going to see it through. No man wants to be labeled a quitter. He would rather go down with the ship than face his peers onshore only to confess his failure for not even attempting to save the ship. Even if he reaches his goal and fails miserably at it, he would rather say "I reached the goal and it didn't work out."

10

Running the Business

Anybody who would say that a relationship isn't like running a business has never been in a real relationship. Everyone I've ever spoken with has professed that it's work. It's a job you come home to. It's a business that runs 24 hours a day and everyday brings about change and uncertainty. It's important to understand the type of business entity you are running. You must also identify the roles of the executive board and the stockholders. Before you do this, you have to know who these individuals are. This isn't hard because we're talking about a relationship between two people - you and him. If there are others, that is going to be a problem. Let's look at these various hats you both must wear.

The board of your organization consists of you and him. Within this mix are at least a president, a vice president, treasurer or comptroller and a secretary. You and he will certainly be at the top as president and VP. In a perfect world the two of you will collaborate and make decisions together. You represent each other in public whether together or apart so you really need to be on the same accord thus representing each other with consistency. One of you will probably be designated the treasurer or comptroller. This role is normally given to the person who is considered to be better with handling the money. It's not uncommon for one person to pay the bills from a joint account. This doesn't mean you can't have your separate spending accounts. That's a whole different ball of wax that people have mixed opinions about.

Side note: I believe it's a problem only when those accounts are hidden from the other person. It becomes a concern of deception. If you're hiding this, what else are you hiding? If you're truly in this thing together, why should anything be a secret?

Now every great organization has a secretary to keep those important meeting notes. This task is generally assumed by the person with the best memory. You're probably not going to sit at a meeting table and discuss every single detail of your relationship, document it and draft a contract. However, somebody is going to have the elephant memory and will inevitably remember just about everything discussed. This can be an advantage and a disadvantage. Let me explain. The secretary is the person who is going to best recall every decision made to the detail. If you are not this person then it's best you say what you mean and mean what you say the first time around. If you try to change on the fly, it's not going to be easy. You will be reminded of your original decision and why it was decided that way. This could lead to a big disagreement unless you can justify the change. Innocently, you may not remember your original decision which is why this person is so crucial.

In my past relationships, I've been on both sides of the coin. I've been the one with the elephant memory and had to threaten to carry a digital recorder to record all of our conversations. Her recall was never accurate and she never remembered what she said but I did. When I reminded her of her words she never agreed. "I never said that," was the typical reply. I've also been that other person. Perhaps it's selective amnesia or perhaps it's just senility setting in. Whatever the case, the secretary plays a vital role in recalling conversations and decisions to help keep the business on track.

Now let's talk about the stakeholders. Who are these people and why are they important. Up to this point you and your mate have worn the hats and now we throw some other folks in the mix. There may be kids or other dependent family members. Your job may be considered a stakeholder along with friends and, yes, the two of you are also stakeholders. You may not agree with me at this moment that each of these people should be considered but let me show you how they are considered stakeholders.

You and your mate are primary stakeholders because whatever happens directly impacts you and filters down to the others. The decisions you make in your relationship and how you run it set the atmosphere for everything else that happens in your life. You don't believe me? Watch this.

Scenario #4: Yesterday afternoon you discovered a possible error in the bank statement to the joint account. You contacted the bank and confirmed that it was a valid transaction for a shoe purchase (yes, men love shoes also). When your husband arrived home, you brought it to his attention over dinner. He admitted to having splurged $300 on a pair of alligator dress shoes without getting your consent. It was an impulse purchase because the shoes were marked way down and they had one pair left in his size. The problem is not that he purchased the shoes but it's that he did it without discussing it with you and taking the money from the joint account. You are hot under the collar and it results in an argument. Admittedly, you say some things that you shouldn't and the situation escalates into a shouting match where you begin to falsely accuse each other of hiding other details. STOP!!

Before I go any further, you now see how one small thing, in this case a $300 pair of shoes, can corrupt an entire relationship. After a long session of shouting your perspectives in an attempt to help the other understand why you're angry, he apologizes and admits his wrong. As with anything that reaches a boiling temperature, you're still furious and will need some time to cool down. Now today you're at work and still thinking about it. Perhaps it's because you saw him head out to work in those nice gators this morning and had a flashback. Now your day is messed up and you can't seem to focus on getting you work done. What is the impact? Well it may be your job. Your productivity is now suffering as a result of what happened at home 12 hours ago.

On your way home, your BFF calls to talk for a while. Little does she know she is entering a war zone as you begin to unload your feeling about yesterday on her. "Girl he was wrong for that. He knows that was bill money and went in it and did not say a word. I don't think he was going to tell me about it at all if I hadn't seen it. What else is he hiding?" She didn't call for that earful but being the friend that she is she listens and even takes sides with you. She's been impacted and now she knows all your business. Who is she going to tell? When will you see this example posted on Facebook?

<u>Side note</u>: Here's a good example of why you need to keep what is going on in your relationship between the two of you. Friends and family will side

with you even when you're wrong and have you believing your thoughts and feelings are justified.

This last example is an example of an emotional stakeholder. What you do hasn't impacted their pocketbooks but you've given them something to think about. Your children can be impacted significantly in the same way so be very careful. Don't make decisions and question them about things that make them choose sides. It's not fair to them and it's certainly not a good gauge as to how good your decision is. They don't know any better.

I need to get back to the business side of things now. As stakeholders yourselves, you obviously have emotional investments but you also have financial investments tied up in this relationship. Though you may or may not live in the same household, you still invest in spending time together (movies, dinner, travel, etc.). What return are you receiving on your investment? Are you making a good investment? Are you investing enough to realize a return? These are questions only you can answer. If you can't answer favorably to any of these, why are you in business/this relationship in the first place?

When I think of how much money I've invested in dating and how those relationships really never went anywhere, it kind of sickens me. I think of how I could have invested a good portion of that money in a retirement account and been sitting pretty when that time comes. Many of you are in the same position but many of you still have plenty of time to assess where you are and what you are doing to decide if your current business arrangement is beneficial to either of you. Who will be the bigger person to say this isn't working and we need help to make it work? Further, who will have the unfavorable job of being the whistleblower that brings this whole operation to a screeching halt?

11

The Sack Don't Seal the Deal

Now finally we come to this "sum it all up" chapter. For those of you who continuously find yourselves trapped in a pool of frustration, there's a good chance that this chapter is just for you. Many women have asked themselves why they keep meeting the same kind of men and why their relationships end shortly after becoming intimate. They want to know what they're doing wrong. I venture to ask those same women what they are doing right. As the saying goes, "If you continue to do what you've always done, expect the same results." There's your answer. Stop doing the same things. Stop going to the same places and you will probably see a difference in the caliber of people you attract. Let's break these two things down.

Stop doing the same things

- Check your lifestyle
- Check the clothing you wear
- Check your conversation
- Check your attitude
- Check your aptitude

These are probably five of the best points nobody has ever given you. Now we can dig a little deeper into these as well. Your lifestyle plays a significant part in the people you attract. Are you a gangster or a holy roller? These are two totally opposite extremes. However, they both attract different types of people for obvious reasons. If you're unsure of the type of person you are you can pretty much find out by checking those who hang around you. Notice I didn't say those you hang around. The difference is you want to see who you're attracting. You could hang with thugs but that doesn't mean you are thug material. It just means that you are attracted to that lifestyle. As a contrast, you could hang with clergymen but that doesn't mean that God had called you to be one of them. So check your company and see who you are attracting. Less the few curious Georges that may hang around you, the majority will rule.

Your attire speaks volumes at a glance. It doesn't necessarily speak to your character and integrity but it does help to formulate an initial opinion about you. If a man who fits the stereotypical mold of homelessness enters a luxury car dealership, it's likely that he wouldn't be quickly approached by sales staff. If the same man enters wearing a suit and donning the stereotypical image of a rich man, most likely sales staff would swarm to his aid. Why is this? It's because we typically judge a book by its cover. If it looks good on the outside then surely there is something to it. What are you wearing when you meet these same kinds of guys? Are you dressing with integrity and character? This is to say that you value your goods and don't believe in being a walking billboard of lust. What message is your clothing sending to others? Is it not possible to be sexy and attractive while wearing less revealing clothing? Even more so, what message are you sending to young ladies who look up to you? Will they follow your lead and succumb to the same fate of never finding Mr. Right because of the messages their clothing sends? I can't answer these questions in this book but hopefully you can and will determine for yourself if a change needs to be made in this area of your life.

What you say is just as important as how you look. In fact the two go hand in hand. If you are polished on the outside, others would only assume that your intellect is just as polished. Nothing is worse than speaking to a woman who appears to have it going on and she is not well spoken. Ladies may say the same about a man. These are the people you don't mind being seen with but you prefer to do all the talking. You just know that if they open their mouths there's no telling what is going to fall out of it. Embarrassment is almost a given in this instance. Understanding the person you are with may help you to improve in this area. If you want to attract a baller, it may be a good idea to speak his language. At least know something about the sport. I'm not saying you have to know more than the commentators but have some idea about what's going on. This shows that you have some level of interest (even if you don't). Remember one of the things a man needs is that support and he should reciprocate. If you're dating a high-profile person, your life is going to equally be under a microscope. Just look at the red carpet in Hollywood. Tabloids love talking about who's dating whom and why. Further, the people want to know what makes you so special. If you can't speak well, there has to be something about you that made him take notice and choose you over the rest. Remember, you are an extension of each other and must learn how to represent each other well.

In many scenes, attitude will get you everywhere but in as many others, it will determine how far you get. Even in your job you may wonder why others are moving ahead but you have more seniority. Notice who they are and why you think they're moving ahead and getting those promotions. Your first thought may be that they're sleeping with the boss. While that may be true, it's also possible that their attitude is different and perhaps this reflects in their work ethic. Somebody obviously took notice. Here is where you may want to do a comparison. Look at your attitude and compare it to theirs. Are you nasty or standoffish? Do you create problems instead of finding resolutions to them? Are you a go to person (leader) or do people stay away from you because of the headaches you cause? Do you take charge and create opportunities or just complain about those who do? This is attitude. While I used this workplace scenario, you can certainly apply this same evaluation to your relationships. Do you create a pleasant atmosphere for your man to come home to or does he find reasons to work late just to avoid coming home? As mentioned previously, men like peace. We despise confusion. Why do you think a man loves his man cave so much? It's where he can escape everyone else in the house and the noise. Men find tranquility in the simplest places - even the bathroom. Does he go in there and stay forever? It may not be directly related to something he's eaten. You probably don't have to look far from self to figure out what is going wrong here.

Last thing is to check your aptitude. This is a simple assessment of where you think you fit in this person's life. If he's a 10 and you're a 2, what do you have to do to step up your game? How do you make him step up and take notice of you not because of your physique but because of your virtue? What do you have that will enhance him. I shared with someone one time and didn't realize the impact it had until he later came to me and reminded me and shared how it impacted his life. What I shared was simple: When a person starts to talk that "I love you and I want you to be a part of my life" stuff, ask them "What value do I add to your life?" If they can't answer this question without stumbling and fumbling to find words, it's obvious they haven't given it much thought and you may want to rethink what you mean to this person. A relationship should enhance not take from. Each person's job should be to please the other and to bring value to their life. When one is tired or weary the other should assist by carrying the load. Each action is reciprocated. What you freely give is what you should freely receive. If you sow discord that shall you also reap. You can't make withdrawals without making deposits. I look at this as a friendly competition to see who can love the best by giving their very best. I'm not referring to material things. Though gifts are wonderful, they still don't make up for the emotional gifts that come with a sentimental note on the kitchen counter to start the day or a sweet note on the pillow to end the evening. Remember the way you show love is individual so just be sure that you communicate this to the other person so they understand that this is your way of telling them how much you care. "I love you" doesn't always have to be audible but can be demonstrated in many ways.

If after reading this, you feel you fall short in any of these areas, you know a change is going to be required to get a man and keep him. Just so it's understood that I'm not picking on the ladies, men can certainly apply the principles as well. I'm just writing and sharing this from a modern day perspective. The things you may have read in other books may reflect ways of handling the problems of yesteryear but this is a new age. Ladies, I felt you needed to hear it from a new age perspective. Certainly everything you've read is my opinion but it has been formed over a number of years of dating the right women and the wrong ones. Much of it is sound advice that I've shared with some of my closest friends over the years to spare them heartache. Since every situation is unique, I encourage you to do a complete assessment of your specific situation before applying any advice from this book or from other individuals.

I realize that this could probably be its own chapter but I want to get back to the title of the chapter. The sack don't seal the deal means just that. Even if you have all these other areas wrong, many times women have this false hope that by sleeping with a man he'll be hers. I can't tell you how wrong you are but I can say you're wrong. Unless a man wants to be with you, sex is all it is. You can wine him and dine him. You can do his laundry and clean his house but if you're not the one, you're not the one. Enough said. Unfortunately for many of you, you don't discover this until after you've slept with him. However, if you rewind conversations you had prior, you'll probably remember him saying something that would have clued you in that he wasn't necessarily considering you a wifey candidate. It's unfortunate but it happens all the time. Open your mouth and keep your legs closed. Talk and listen. Sex is not going to make him fall head over heels in love with you and it's certainly not going to make him put a ring on your hand. How long does it take may not be the question you should be asking right now. Is he most interested in being the man to keep that smile on your face or is he more interested in the moisture between your thighs. This is the question you want him to answer. Pay close attention and he WILL answer it. Just remember you can't complain about the things you ALLOW him to do.

12

Stop Juicing His Head Up

If he's a dud, he's a dud. Call a spade a spade. Men have their own way of doing the same thing when we meet a woman who is lousy in bed. While most people don't want to be the bearer of bad news, sometimes you just can't help yourself. For example, what if it happens and he is lousy and you don't want to be bothered? You may not call him but he'll call you. You'll ignore his calls until he stops and you think he got the message. Then one day while out and about, you run into him but he sees you before you see him and you attempt an escape. Now here comes the discussion because he'll want to know why you didn't call. Truth is he really knows but he also knows that you would never tell the truth so he's comfortable receiving the answer you give him "I've been super busy."

Noooooo!!!! Here's your second chance to tell him that he's a great guy but you realized that you weren't compatible. By doing so you eliminate having to revisit this conversation again when you run into him again because inevitably, you will. You don't have to be specific and he probably won't ask because his ego is already shattered at this point by the mere fact you didn't call him back. He wants to save face so he probably won't make mention of the sex. He may dance around that and say that he thought you enjoyed the conversation and hanging out as much as he did. He's really saying that he enjoyed the sex and really doesn't want to miss an opportunity to do it again. When all the other small talk fails he then may make mention of the intimacy and have a few excuses for his ill performance to pull out of his back pocket in hopes that you'll give him a second chance to redeem himself. Now the ball's in your court –no pun intended. You'll have to make a decision at this point on whether there will be a round two.

Round two normally means one of two things. It was good enough the first time to warrant another or it's a redemption round. If you opt for the redemption round, he's probably not going to know the difference. He'll be thinking round one was a stellar performance unless you tell him which most women will not. This takes me to the title of the chapter. Why juice up his head?. If he sucks let him know. Right now there are so many arrogant brothers walking God's green earth with their heads in the clouds because some woman "oooh awwwed" too many times and made them think they were gods. This, ladies, is a big mistake. While Biblically we shouldn't be indulging anyway before marriage, if you have succumbed to the power of the wood (y'all know what I'm talking about) and you faked it then you are dead wrong. I've asked this question many times of women. Why do you fake it? Who is this benefitting? Most say it's to keep from hurting his ego and then some say it's to get him off of me as quickly as possible. I don't know which it may have been for you but faking is the wrong thing to do.

If you determine that he's the one you want to be with despite his performance in this area, then a conversation should be had on how to improve the experience for both of you. Yes I said both because this will help that "save face" moment if you take some of the flack; he won't feel like he's inadequate and alone in this even though he probably is.

Side Note: This, gentlemen, is one of those moments that you can use to your benefit as well if she's coming up a little short on the pleasuring end. Consider it a freebie for you guys.

Truthfully, a man's ego is going to be hurt more if he finds out later that you were faking it. Let's not even mention if you were to step outside of the relationship and he finds out. How devastating would that be if he discovers that what you were missing is something he would have willingly provided had he known? Communication is the key even when it comes to sex - before and after it happens.

Don't assume he or she knows it all. While some are skilled in various areas, others are not. Everybody knows that what's good for the goose is not necessarily good for the gander. You cannot expect him to know your body if he hasn't had the time to learn it. Unfortunately, many women don't take the time to get to know their own bodies but will talk a man down if he doesn't. Ladies, you're dead wrong for this. Your man shouldn't know your body better than you. He should get to know it as well as you but if you don't take the time, why should he. I'm not endorsing masturbation so don't jump up and flood the toy stores. I'm sure they would appreciate it but my point is not to get a toy and go to work on yourself. The point I'm making is to not beat a man up for not knowing how to touch you when the reality is you don't know how to be touched.

Now back to the title. You have to be real to yourself. For those of you who know what you like and may be a bit more seasoned in your sexuality than some of your peers, it's ok to turn a guy down and let him know that it's best you remain friends and nothing more. If he asks, be honest with him. If he wants to go even deeper and asks for a critique, please share. An informed brother who is genuinely interested in being a better lover is not going to be afraid to ask "What can I do to be a better lover?" Even though it may be too late for the two of you to work it out, his mere concern to do better by the next woman is a testament that he cares about someone more than himself. A selfish lover he probably isn't.

Now let's summarize what we've learned here. Stop faking it!! It doesn't benefit either of you. Be honest about your likes and dislikes. If you aren't compatible in simple discussion, you know it's not going to work under the sheets, on the kitchen counter, in the living room or wherever else you try to get it in. If by a lucky chance he asks you to critique him, be as honest as possible. This is where the gloves come off. He asked for it. This doesn't mean be nasty and offensive but it does mean give him good, honest feedback. I know what some of you are doing at this very moment. You're shaking your head and saying "Why would I give him that so he can do it better with the next woman?" The answer is simple: He asked you to. If you're thinking this right now, then you are probably the selfish one who would never ask for such critique. You think you have it all together and every man wants you. You're probably only in it for yourself. That being said, maybe he isn't the problem. Maybe it's your high and mighty attitude that makes him not want to be a great lover to you. Hmmmmm. Your thoughts?.......(crickets)

13

He's Not Pursuing You!

One too many times I've had this discussion with my female friends wanting to know how they'll know if a guy is interested. My reply: You already know. However, it's again a case of knowing but not wanting to accept the reality. It's all a part of fear and not wanting to feel rejected. I get this since nobody likes rejection. However, if you don't own it, you'll be hurt by it and this happens way too often.

Scenario 5: You meet a great guy. He approaches you and he has great conversation. We must note his approach from the very beginning wasn't "Wow, how can I get to know you?" It was subtle. He approached and introduced himself and conversation continued from there. The obvious is that he thought enough of you to approach so clearly he is interested in something. It's up to you to now find out what that something is. To do this is not to ask him "What do you want from me?" No that would be defensive and a terrible assumption that he wants anything more than conversation. However, if you get beyond this initial conversation, at some point his intentions will be revealed or you can ask at that time, but not yet. You discover some common interests and agree to exchange numbers. A couple of days later he calls to say hello and you converse for a little while. So far everything is great and here is where most women begin to assume that he is really digging them and begin to change. Without knowing or even having a discussion about what his intent is, and after two conversations you assume he is pursuing you. He asks you out one evening and you have a great time. A couple of weekends later he asks you out again and your suspicion is even more solidified.

So far you've gone out twice and conversation is good but what I haven't revealed is how general your conversations have been and I do mean general. You really haven't discussed anything specific but YOU are all ready to jump the gun. STOP!! You need to have that specific discussion. Where is this going? Do you have any specific intentions since we've been spending quite a bit of time together? You may be surprised to discover that he thinks you're a great woman and is enjoying the time you're spending but is not interested in a commitment. What he is interested in is a companion. He wants to have somebody to simply hang out with and talk to without pressure. Probably not what you want to hear since you really like him but knowing this truth will spare your feelings and help you make intelligent decisions as your friendship develops. At this point you may even decide to bow out gracefully, explaining that you really don't need any more friends and are looking for something more. I don't recommend this because you're giving up on, if nothing more, a potentially great friendship. Who's to say that his mind may not change later and you could be the lucky lady? This has happened to me on numerous occasions but I'm glad to say that most got over it and we're great friends today. Okay, I digress. However, it is decision time for you. Knowing what you now know about him not wanting a commitment, will you sleep with him? Will you confide in him? How close will you allow yourself to get to him knowing that your efforts may be futile? After all, what you really want is a commitment that has the potential of leading to marriage, a family and bliss, right?

Men fall into one of three categories when it comes to a woman. Here's the simple rule of thumb. If he asks you out periodically and limits conversation to general discussion, he's probably not pursuing you. If you go out regularly and conversation has graduated from general to being more specific and personal then it's reasonable to assess that he is considering pursuing you. Notice I said considering. Now once the conversation becomes and remains personal, it's likely that he **IS** in pursuit. Let me outline them here.

- **General** – Conversation is general discussions about politics, life, self, etc., with periodic non-romantic encounters (I dare not call them dates)

- **Consideration of Pursuit** – Regular encounters (again, not dates) and graduated conversations about things such as goals, family and past experiences

- **Pursuit** – Regular encounters (safe to call them dates now) with more personal discussions about relationship likes and dislikes, romance, sex and even discussions about marriage

I reiterate that if at any point in this discovery period you have questions, ask. I can't stress this enough. It's important to not assume. You'll save face and heartache by doing so. Unfortunately, most women get in their feelings way too soon and before giving any of this any real consideration. The answers to most of your questions, ladies, are right in front of you if you acknowledge them for what they are. As the saying goes, "Iif it looks like a duck and quacks like a duck, it's a duck."

Above all, stop asking him. If he wants you, he'll let you know it; he'll say it and he'll show it. Your asking him will drive him away, especially if all he really desires with you is a friendship. It's cute at first but it really becomes pestering and will cause him to withdraw from you completely with your feelings in mind. Men know that if they get too close (or allow you to) it will impact you emotionally. Believe it or not, there are men that have your best interest at heart. If he tells you that he's not interested, listen to him. Do what you must to guard your heart at this point. If you get caught up, it's nobody's fault but yours at this point. Of course men will always be blamed for your hurt but let's look at the reality of it. He told you, you didn't listen, now you're hurt. Really? Who's at fault?

14

Play By Your Own Rules

What are your rules or have you played by everyone else's rules so long that you've forgotten to create your own? That's what happens to many of us. We cater to others so much that we lose ourselves. It's not until we are up in age that we realize what we've done and decide to try and live the life we have left doing what we want to do. This isn't just true in relationships but in everyday life. Parents do it all the time. We give up our dreams and ambitions to focus on the children. Perhaps this is more justified than losing yourself in a relationship with a potential mate or spouse. However, we're going to focus on the relationship aspect.

I always say if you don't know, don't assume. Ask. I told a friend to ask a guy she was interested in a series of questions. She said he may become offended and feel as if he was being interrogated. That's not quite the term I would use but is that not what we're doing when we're getting to know someone? We ask questions. Only a person attempting to hide something is going to be offended by your questions. Why else wouldn't they be candid enough to entertain it? Ladies you must ask questions. She told me that she finds herself adjusting to his comfort level and meeting him on his terms. Therefore she doesn't poke or probe or simply ask basic questions. This is when I told her that she has been playing by a man's rules too long and to create her own.

Ladies you have to play by your rules. Stop adjusting. If he doesn't like the way you play, he can find another playmate. Never should you sacrifice your morals, values, integrity or happiness to cater to his ego or bend to the tradition that you should play by his rules. No! The game has changed. You do have the right to be happy on your terms. Stop compromising in fear that if you don't you'll grow old and lonely. I concur you will grow old and there may be some lonely moments in or out of a relationship but in either case, you can still be happy. You can be happy knowing you did it your way and that you didn't jeopardize your values to get a man.

I meet so many successful, single women who say that guys are intimidated by their success. To this I say, congratulations. You avoided a messy situation. Why? I say this because a man who is intimidated by a woman's success has control issues. He can't handle her success for fear that she will run the show. Now in their defense, women can make a man feel that way at times. I've seen it. Just because you are successful doesn't mean you should wear the pants. There is certain responsibility that should be relinquished to a man. This doesn't make you a weak-minded person. It actually shows that you know when to allow a man to be a man. A real man will respect this and step to the plate because it gives him a sense of value in your life. I realize also that many of you have done it alone for so long that it may be difficult for you to relinquish some of this responsibility but I can tell you that the sooner you become accustomed to doing so, the more value your man is going to feel and the more he's going to show you how much he appreciates it.

It's important to be comfortable and confident in who you are and it's ok for it to show. Confidence is sexy and attractive. It only repulses those it should. Understand there's a difference between confident and cocky. Confidence gets attention. It's what silences a room and makes people take note when you enter. Your confidence can set the tone for a meeting and gives people the desire to follow you. Just as wealthy people surround themselves with other wealthy people. Confident people tend to embrace opportunities to meet other like minded people. Each of these groups gathers strength from one another. Weak, controlling people have a need to feel superior. Understanding that they would never make it in either of these other groups, they tend to seek out weaker individuals they can control to make themselves appear superior. This is why so many women find themselves in abusive relationships. At some point their abuser decided that using violence and harsh words was going to be the means by which he would ensure that he maintained control in the relationship. Personally it's a punk move. There are ways to deal with this. My mom would have called it a frying pan back in the day. Today there are others but I will leave those to your own discretion.

To get back to the topic, ladies you have your own opinion. Never let a man change that. You have your own desires, never make his, yours. You have your own dreams and ambitions. Never sacrifice those for his. Relationships are about working together and compromise. There is nothing about a relationship that says "you will like what I like and do what I say." That is a dictatorship. When you come across any man who demonstrates these characteristics I beseech you to get out early. A relationship like that is destined to produce problems and you will never realize true happiness or reach your true potential fooling around with him. Remember, once a controlling man takes control, it will be hard for him to let go and even harder for you to break away if he won't let go.

15

He Wants A Strong Woman

He says he wants a strong woman but what does that mean? In most conversations when this question comes up "What do you want in a woman?" the typical reply is "I want a strong woman." Is there really a single definition for strong woman? There are numerous examples of what a strong woman is but way too many to list in so few pages of this book. I venture to say that this means something different to each individual. To some men a strong woman may mean emotionally stable, employed and independent. To others it may simply mean a homemaker, good mother and God fearing. The best thing to do when a man replies this way is to ask him what that means to him.

This is a good conversation to have before you begin telling a man the things you desire in a mate. In my book literally and figuratively, this is a big no-no. People will become who they think you want them to be. In other words, if I tell you that I'm looking for xyz in a woman then you will become those things, at least temporarily. Everyone knows you can only where a mask for so long and eventually the real you is going to come shining through. So rather than say what I'm looking for, I prefer to watch and learn. If you recall, I stated earlier in the book that so much can be learned through observation and without saying a word. However, in this case asking him what he means when he makes this statement will help you understand what a strong woman is in his eyes.

Don't be afraid to ask questions. You need to identify what his expectations are of you if he makes you a part of his life. You need to do the same. There are desires and then there are expectations in relationships. It's up to both parties to be candid about both and be truthful, especially to you. If you can't be what that person needs you to be then be honest and bold enough to walk. It's for this reason that many people find themselves in jacked up relationships later. You knew all along that you weren't right for that person but you chose to stick around and make their life miserable. Now you're miserable trying to be somebody you're not. It gets real messy later so why not deal with it from the very beginning.

16

The Beginning, Not the Conclusion

Relationships are hard because we make them hard. Though we're individual, we have common needs. We also have unique ways of giving and receiving love. Understanding the people we deal with is the key to all successful relationships. This takes more than just one date. Married couples will tell you that it's work that you come home to. Relationships involve the never-ending effort of getting to know someone. It's not something you just do one time and it's done. Changing times cause us to evolve so we will always be getting to know each other. It's uncomfortable sometimes, but necessary. We have to determine if we want to assist each other with jumping over the hurdles of life to get to a beautiful place or if we want to exit the race and forfeit opportunities to achieve great things – together.

10 Things You Should Know & Do

1. Choose ye this day what it is you truly desire.
2. Understand what it is the other person desires and determine if you are willing to help them meet that desire.
3. Be honest.
4. Let your intentions be made known up front and save time.
5. Don't receive more than you're willing to give.
6. Recognize that it's going to take effort.
7. Don't give up so quickly. Building a solid foundation that won't wash away when the storms come is imperative.
8. Keep others away!! This is between the two of you. Listening to outsiders is one quick way to sabotage your relationship.
9. Don't let material things determine a person's value in your eyes. They could be broke tomorrow.
10. Understand that one night of passion does not mean he's yours forever.
11. Don't compromise; be true to you and follow your own rules.

NOTES

NOTES

I hope this book has proven to be exactly what I said it would be as you begin to understand men in a whole new way.

Proverbs 4:7 – New Living Translation
"Getting wisdom is the wisest thing you can do! And whatever else you do, develop good judgment."

CPSIA information can be obtained at www.ICGtesting.com
Printed in the USA
LVOW12s1433111013

356554LV00002B/377/P